T0126586

THE LITTLE BOOK OF
THE ART OF
WAR

Published by OH!
20 Mortimer Street
London W1T 3JW

Disclaimer:

ISBN 978-1-91161-063-2

Editorial: Alex Lemon
Project manager: Russell Porter
Design: Tony Seddon
Production: Rachel Burgess

A CIP catalogue record for this book is available from the British Library

Printed in Dubai

10 9 8 7 6 5 4 3 2 1

THE LITTLE BOOK OF
THE ART OF WAR

STRATEGIES TO LIVE BY

CONTENTS

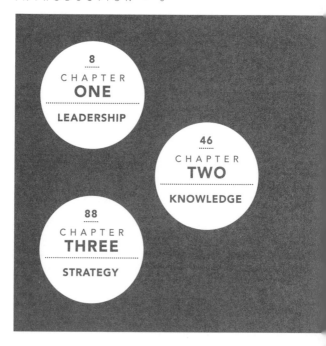

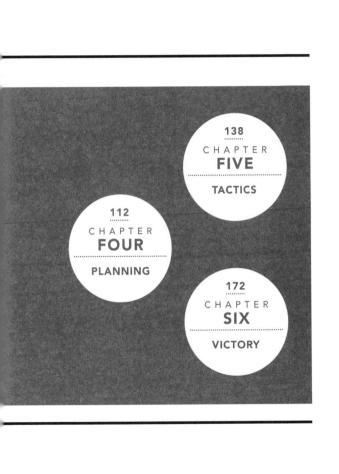

INTRODUCTION

The Art of War originated in China 2,500 years ago, but its influence has reached across the centuries, around the world and far beyond the military.

Believed to have been written by military strategist and philosopher Sun Tzu in the fifth century BC, it's packed with wisdom on all aspects of winning in war, from weaponry and supplies to the terrain of battle and energy of troops.

But what makes this ancient book about battle relevant to modern life is its advice on setting the right goals, avoiding confrontation, outsmarting opponents, leading a team and maintaining morale.

The Art of War has long been important to East Asian leaders, but its influence only began to travel west when it was translated into French in the late 1700s. A full English translation didn't appear until the early 1900s.

As the twentieth century wore on, *The Art of War* informed and inspired leaders in modern conflicts. Mao Zedong was said to use it in winning the Chinese Civil War. World War Two commander US General MacArthur kept a copy on his desk. General "Stormin'" Norman Schwarzkopf drew on its teachings to fight the Gulf War.

Today, *The Art of War* is name-checked far from the ancient battlefield, in sports teams, in business meetings and in pop culture. Record-breaking Super Bowl coaches refer to it, Tony Soprano tells his shrink he's reading it, and it's cited in numerous books and articles guiding CEOs, marketing executives and start-up founders.

Now *The Little Book of The Art of War* gathers together the nuggets of knowledge most relevant to our world, compressing the text's original thirteen chapters under six new headings: leadership, knowledge, strategy, planning, tactics and victory.

Dip in, absorb, apply and get ahead in life today using the strategic know-how of the ancient commanders.

孫子
兵法

CHAPTER
ONE

LEADERSHIP

No group of people, whether army or team, will succeed in its aims without strong leadership. *The Art of War*'s chapters contain numerous words of wisdom on the attributes, knowledge and character that make a good leader, about the behaviours and actions that make a good leader great, and about the faults that can trip up even the most determined figurehead.

孫子兵法

The Commander stands for the virtues of wisdom, sincerity, benevolence, courage and strictness.

"

The leader of armies is the
arbiter of the people's fate,
the man on whom it depends
whether the nation shall be in
peace or in peril.

"

孫子兵法

> **"**
>
> The highest form of generalship is to balk the enemy's plans.
>
> **"**

66

To see victory only when it is within the ken of the common herd is not the acme of excellence.

99

孫子兵法

> **The consummate leader cultivates the moral law, and strictly adheres to method and discipline; thus it is in his power to control success.**

66

The control of a large force
is the same principle as the
control of a few men: it is
merely a question of dividing
up their numbers.

99

孫子兵法

> **"**
> The quality of decision is
> like the well-timed swoop
> of a falcon which enables
> it to strike and destroy its
> victim.
> **"**

"

Energy may
be likened to the
bending of a crossbow;
decision, to the
releasing of
a trigger.

"

孫子兵法

"

The clever combatant looks to
the effect of combined energy,
and does not require too much
from individuals.

"

66

Maneuvering with an army is advantageous; with an undisciplined multitude, most dangerous.

99

孫子兵法

> The host thus forming a single united body, it is impossible either for the brave to advance alone, or for the cowardly to retreat alone. This is the art of handling large masses of men.

"

A whole army may be robbed of its spirit; a commander-in-chief may be robbed of his presence of mind.

"

孫子兵法

❝

The general who thoroughly understands the advantages that accompany variation of tactics knows how to handle his troops.

❞

66

There are five dangerous faults which may affect a general: recklessness, which leads to destruction; cowardice, which leads to capture; a hasty temper, which can be provoked by insults; a delicacy of honor, which is sensitive to shame; over-solicitude for his men, which exposes him to worry and trouble.

99

孫子兵法

> 66
>
> If soldiers are punished before they have grown attached to you, they will not prove submissive; and, unless submissive, then will be practically useless.
>
> 99

66

If, when the soldiers have become attached to you, punishments are not enforced, they will still be useless.

99

孫子兵法

66

Soldiers must be treated
in the first instance with
humanity, but kept under
control by means of iron
discipline. This is a certain
road to victory.

99

"

If in training soldiers
commands are habitually
enforced, the army will be
well-disciplined; if not, its
discipline will be bad.

"

孫子兵法

> **"** If a general shows confidence in his men but always insists on his orders being obeyed, the gain will be mutual. **"**

66

When the common soldiers are too strong and their officers too weak, the result is insubordination.

99

孫子兵法

> **66**
>
> When the officers are too strong and the common soldiers too weak, the result is collapse.
>
> **99**

"

When the higher officers are angry and insubordinate, and on meeting the enemy give battle on their own account from a feeling of resentment, before the commander-in-chief can tell whether or not he is in a position to fight, the result is ruin.

"

孫子兵法

> **"** When the general is weak and without authority; when his orders are not clear and distinct; when there are no fixed duties assigned to officers and men, and the ranks are formed in a slovenly haphazard manner, the result is utter disorganization. **"**

66

When a general, unable to
estimate the enemy's strength,
allows an inferior force to
engage a larger one, or hurls
a weak detachment against
a powerful one, and neglects
to place picked soldiers in
the front rank, the result
must be rout.

99

孫子兵法

> ## 66
>
> The general who
> advances without
> coveting fame and
> retreats without
> fearing disgrace ...
> is the jewel of
> the kingdom.
>
> ## 99

66

A power of estimating the adversary, of controlling the forces of victory, and of shrewdly calculating difficulties, dangers and distances, constitutes the test of a great general.

99

孫子兵法

***

66

Regard your soldiers as your children, and they will follow you into the deepest valleys; look upon them as your own beloved sons, and they will stand by you even unto death.

99

66

If ... you are indulgent, but unable to make your authority felt; kind-hearted, but unable to enforce your commands; and incapable, moreover, of quelling disorder: then your soldiers must be likened to spoilt children; they are useless for any practical purpose.

99

孫子兵法

> Those who were called skillful leaders of old knew how to drive a wedge between the enemy's front and rear; to prevent co-operation between his large and small divisions; to hinder the good troops from rescuing the bad, the officers from rallying their men.

66

The principle on which to manage an army is to set up one standard of courage which all must reach.

99

孫子兵法

It is the business of a general to be quiet, and thus ensure secrecy; upright and just, and thus maintain order.

"

Bestow rewards without regard to rule, issue orders without regard to previous arrangements; and you will be able to handle a whole army as though you had to do with but a single man.

"

孫子兵法

> Confront your soldiers
> with the deed itself; never
> let them know your design.
> When the outlook is bright,
> bring it before their eyes; but
> tell them nothing when the
> situation is gloomy.

Be stern in the
council-chamber, so
that you may control
the situation.

孫子兵法

66

No ruler should put troops
into the field merely to gratify
his own spleen; no general
should fight a battle simply
out of pique.

99

66

The enlightened ruler is heedful and the good general full of caution. This is the way to keep a country at peace and an army intact.

99

孫子兵法

CHAPTER
TWO

KNOWLEDGE

"Know your enemy" is a well known saying and one that appears early in the *The Art of War*. But its teachings also highlight that your enemy isn't the only thing you need knowledge on, and that they won't be the only opposition you'll face in achieving your aims. From terrain to behaviours, to alliances to oneself, Sun Tzu had plenty of advice about what you need to know about to emerge the victor.

孫子兵法

66

If you know the enemy
and know yourself, you
need not fear the result of
a hundred battles.

99

66

If you know yourself but not the enemy, for every victory gained you will also suffer a defeat.

99

孫子兵法

> **"**
>
> If you know neither the
> enemy nor yourself,
> you will succumb in
> every battle.
>
> **"**

66

By discovering the enemy's
dispositions and remaining
invisible ourselves, we can
keep our forces concentrated,
while the enemy's must be
divided.

99

孫子兵法

> **"** Though the enemy be stronger in numbers, we may prevent him from fighting. Scheme so as to discover his plans and the likelihood of their success. **"**

"

Rouse [the enemy], and learn the principle of his activity or inactivity. Force him to reveal himself, so as to find out his vulnerable spots.

"

孫子兵法

66

We cannot enter
into alliances until
we are acquainted
with the designs of
our neighbours.

99

66

We are not fit to lead an army on the march unless we are familiar with the face of the country.

99

孫子兵法

We shall be unable to turn
natural advantage to account
unless we make use of local
guides.

"

Now a soldier's spirit is keenest in the morning; by noonday it has begun to flag; and in the evening, his mind is bent only on returning to camp.

"

孫子兵法

> 66
>
> A clever general... avoids an army when its spirit is keen, but attacks it when it is sluggish and inclined to return. This is the art of studying moods.
>
> 99

66

Disciplined and calm, to await the appearance of disorder and hubbub amongst the enemy – this is the art of retaining self-possession.

99

孫子兵法

> **66**
>
> To refrain from intercepting an enemy whose banners are in perfect order, to refrain from attacking an army drawn up in calm and confident array – this is the art of studying circumstances.
>
> **99**

All armies prefer high
ground to low and
sunny places to dark.

孫子兵法

66

When the enemy is close
at hand and remains quiet,
he is relying on the natural
strength of his position.

99

66

When [the enemy] keeps aloof
and tries to provoke a battle,
he is anxious for the other side
to advance.

99

孫子兵法

> **66**
>
> Startled beasts
> indicate that a sudden
> attack is coming.
>
> **99**

"

Humble words and increased preparations are signs that the enemy is about to advance. Violent language and driving forward as if to the attack are signs that he will retreat.

"

孫子兵法

> Peace proposals unaccompanied by a sworn covenant indicate a plot.

"

When there is much running about and the soldiers fall into rank, it means that the critical moment has come.

"

孫子兵法

> **"**
>
> When some are seen advancing and some retreating, it is a lure.
>
> **"**

66

If the enemy sees an
advantage to be gained
and makes no effort to
secure it, the soldiers are
exhausted.

99

孫子兵法

> **"** If there is disturbance in the camp, the general's authority is weak. **"**

66

The sight of men whispering together in small knots or speaking in subdued tones points to disaffection amongst the rank and file.

99

孫子兵法

> **"**
> Too frequent rewards
> signify that the enemy is
> at the end of his resources;
> too many punishments
> betray a condition of dire
> distress.
> **"**

"

To begin by bluster, but afterwards to take fright at the enemy's numbers, shows a supreme lack of intelligence.

"

孫子兵法

> **"**
>
> When envoys are sent with compliments in their mouths, it is a sign that the enemy wishes for a truce.
>
> **"**

"

An army is exposed to six several calamities, not arising from natural causes, but from faults for which the general is responsible: flight; insubordination; collapse; ruin; disorganization; rout.

"

孫子兵法

If one force is hurled against another ten times its size, the result will be the flight of the former.

66

The experienced soldier,
once in motion, is never
bewildered; once he has
broken camp, he is never
at a loss.

99

孫子兵法

66

Ground on which we can only
be saved from destruction
by fighting without delay, is
desperate ground.

99

Carefully study the
well-being of your
men, and do not
overtax them.

孫子兵法

> **"**
> We cannot enter into alliance
> with neighboring princes until
> we are acquainted with their
> designs.
> **"**

66

Anger may in time change
to gladness; vexation may be
succeeded by content.

99

孫子兵法

> **66**
>
> A kingdom that has once been destroyed can never come again into being; nor can the dead ever be brought back to life.
>
> **99**

66

What enables the wise
sovereign and the good
general to strike and conquer,
and achieve things beyond
the reach of ordinary men,
is foreknowledge.

99

孫子兵法

> **"**
>
> Knowledge of the enemy's dispositions can only be obtained from other men.
>
> **"**

"

None in the whole army are more intimate relations to be maintained than with spies. None should be more liberally rewarded. In no other business should greater secrecy be preserved.

"

孫子兵法

> **"**
> Spies cannot be usefully
> employed without a certain
> intuitive sagacity. They
> cannot be properly managed
> without benevolence and
> straightforwardness. Without
> subtle ingenuity of mind, one
> cannot make certain of the
> truth of their reports.
> **"**

66

Be subtle! be subtle! and use
your spies for every kind of
business.

99

孫子
兵法
....
CHAPTER
THREE

STRATEGY

Winning the war and not just the
battle isn't about what you do, but
how and why you do it. Central to
The Art of War is the notion that
strength of force comes from unity
not size, and using that strength
to take advantage of an opponent's
weaknesses is the pathway to success.
Develop a clear strategy to unify your
team and exploit your advantages,
and victory is yours.

孫子兵法

> The skillful leader subdues the enemy's troops without any fighting; he captures their cities without laying siege to them; he overthrows their kingdom without lengthy operations in the field.

❝

All warfare is based on deception.

❞

孫子兵法

> **❝**
>
> Hold out baits to entice the enemy. Feign disorder, and crush him.
>
> **❞**

66

Though we have heard of stupid haste in war, cleverness has never been seen associated with long delays.

99

孫子兵法

66

Though an obstinate fight may be made by a small force, in the end it must be captured by the larger force.

99

66

Simulated disorder postulates perfect discipline; simulated fear postulates courage; simulated weakness postulates strength.

99

孫子兵法

> **"** One who is skillful at keeping the enemy on the move maintains deceitful appearances, according to which the enemy will act. **"**

66

Standing on
the defensive
indicates insufficient
strength; attacking, a
superabundance
of strength.

99

孫子兵法

> ## 66
>
> The energy developed by good fighting men is as the momentum of a round stone rolled down a mountain thousands of feet in height.
>
> ## 99

66

The clever combatant imposes his will on the enemy, but does not allow the enemy's will to be imposed on him.

99

孫子兵法

> **"**
>
> In war, the way is to avoid what is strong and to strike at what is weak.
>
> **"**

"

Appear at points which the enemy must hasten to defend; march swiftly to places where you are not expected.

"

孫子兵法

> **"**
>
> O divine art of subtlety and
> secrecy! Through you we
> learn to be invisible, through
> you inaudible; and hence we
> can hold the enemy's fate in
> our hands.
>
> **"**

66

In making tactical dispositions, the highest pitch you can attain is to conceal them; conceal your dispositions, and you will be safe from the prying of the subtlest spies, from the machinations of the wisest brains.

99

孫子兵法

> **The difficulty of tactical manoeuvring consists in turning the devious into the direct, and misfortune into gain.**

66

Do not linger in dangerously isolated positions. In hemmed-in situations, you must resort to stratagem. In desperate position, you must fight.

99

孫子兵法

"

The art of war teaches us to rely not on the likelihood of the enemy's not coming, but on our own readiness to receive him; not on the chance of his not attacking, but rather on the fact that we have made our position unassailable.

"

66

If our troops are no more in number than the enemy, that is amply sufficient; it only means that no direct attack can be made.

99

孫子兵法

66

The further you penetrate into a country, the greater will be the solidarity of your troops, and thus the defenders will not prevail against you.

99

66

If ... in the midst of difficulties we are always ready to seize an advantage, we may extricate ourselves from misfortune.

99

孫子兵法

> By altering his arrangements and changing his plans, [a general] keeps the enemy without definite knowledge. By shifting his camp and taking circuitous routes, he prevents the enemy from anticipating his purpose.

___

66

By persistently hanging on the enemy's flank, we shall succeed in the long run in killing the commander-in-chief.

99

___

孫子兵法

CHAPTER

FOUR

PLANNING

Once you've got your strategy in place, it's time to make a plan. Or maybe even several. Because in Sun Tzu's view, flexibility in the face of changing circumstances is one of the cornerstones of success. When you know what you'll do, you can act swiftly, decisively and deliberately to get ahead and stay there.

孫子兵法

66

When able to attack, we must seem unable; when using our forces, we must seem inactive; when we are near, we must make the enemy believe we are far away; when far away, we must make him believe we are near.

99

"

The general who wins a battle makes many calculations in his temple before the battle is fought. The general who loses a battle makes but few calculations beforehand.

"

孫子兵法

> **"**
>
> According as circumstances are favorable, one should modify one's plans.
>
> **"**

66

When you engage in actual fighting, if victory is long in coming, then men's weapons will grow dull and their ardor will be damped.

99

孫子兵法

> The skillful soldier does not raise a second levy, neither are his supply-wagons loaded more than twice.

"

The skillful fighter puts himself into a position which makes defeat impossible, and does not miss the moment for defeating the enemy.

"

孫子兵法

66

An army may march great
distances without distress, if
it marches through country
where the enemy is not.

99

"

The spot where we intend to fight must not be made known; for then the enemy will have to prepare against a possible attack at several different points.

"

孫子兵法

> **Numerical weakness comes from having to prepare against possible attacks, numerical strength from compelling our adversary to make these preparations against us.**

66

Do not repeat the
tactics which have
gained you one victory,
but let your methods
be regulated by the
infinite variety of
circumstances.

99

孫子兵法

> **"**
> Carefully compare the
> opposing army with your
> own, so that you may
> know where strength is
> superabundant and where
> it is deficient.
> **"**

"

Just as water retains no constant shape, so in warfare there are no constant conditions.

"

孫子兵法

> **66**
>
> An army without its
> baggage-train is lost; without
> provisions it is lost; without
> bases of supply it is lost.
>
> **99**

Ponder and deliberate before you make a move.

孫子兵法

Whether to concentrate or to divide your troops must be decided by circumstances.

66

The student of war who is
unversed in the art of war
of varying his plans ... will
fail to make the best use of
his men.

99

孫子兵法

66

Let your plans be dark and impenetrable as night, and when you move, fall like a thunderbolt.

99

66

In the wise leader's plans,
considerations of advantage
and of disadvantage will be
blended together.

99

孫子兵法

"

He who exercises no
forethought but makes light
of his opponents is sure to be
captured by them.

"

66

There is a proper season
for making attacks with fire,
and special days for starting
a conflagration.

99

孫子兵法

66

Unhappy is the fate of one
who tries to win his battles
and succeed in his attacks
without cultivating the spirit
of enterprise; for the result
is waste of time and general
stagnation.

99

Concentrate your
energy and hoard
your strength.

孫子兵法

> **The enlightened ruler lays his plans well ahead; the good general cultivates his resources.**

66

Move not unless you see an advantage; use not your troops unless there is something to be gained; fight not unless the position is critical.

99

孫子兵法

CHAPTER
FIVE

TACTICS

With a clear strategy and good planning, you're ready for the action of battle. And for the inaction of evasion. Because according to *The Art of War*, winning doesn't just result from deciding where, when and how to attack your enemy, but from deciding whether you need to strike at all. Knowing which direct and indirect tactics to employ is the key to maintaining strength and advantage.

孫子兵法

> 66
>
> To ensure that your whole host may withstand the brunt of the enemy's attack and remain unshaken – this is effected by manoeuvres direct and indirect.
>
> 99

❝

In all fighting, the direct
method may be used for
joining battle, but indirect
methods will be needed in
order to secure victory.

❞

孫子兵法

> **"**
> Indirect tactics, efficiently
> applied, are inexhaustible
> and streams; like the sun and
> moon, they end but to begin
> anew; like the four seasons,
> they pass away to return
> once more.
> **"**

"

In battle, there are not more than two methods of attack – the direct and the indirect; yet these two in combination give rise to an endless series of manoeuvres.

"

孫子兵法

> ##
>
> The direct and the indirect lead on to each other in turn. It is like moving in a circle – you never come to an end.
>
> ##

If he is secure at all points, be prepared for him. If he is in superior strength, evade him.

孫子兵法

"

If [the enemy] is taking his ease, give him no rest. If his forces are united, separate them.

"

"

The captured soldiers should be kindly treated and kept. This is called, using the conquered foe to augment one's own strength.

"

孫子兵法

> **"**
>
> Attack him where
> he is unprepared,
> appear where you
> are not expected.
>
> **"**

> "
>
> It is the rule in war, if our forces are ten to the enemy's one, to surround him; if five to one, to attack him; if twice as numerous, to divide our army into two.
>
> "

孫子兵法

> 66
>
> If equally matched, we can offer battle; if slightly inferior in numbers, we can avoid the enemy; if quite unequal in every way, we can flee from him.
>
> 99

> **Whoever is first in the field and awaits the coming of the enemy, will be fresh for the fight; whoever is second in the field and has to hasten to battle will arrive exhausted.**

孫子兵法

66

By holding out advantages to
him, he can cause the enemy
to approach of his own accord;
or, by inflicting damage, he
can make it impossible for the
enemy to draw near.

99

66

You may advance and be absolutely irresistible, if you make for the enemy's weak points; you may retire and be safe from pursuit if your movements are more rapid than those of the enemy.

99

孫子兵法

> **"**
> If we wish to fight, the enemy can be forced to an engagement ... All we need do is attack some other place that he will be obliged to relieve.
> **"**

Let your rapidity
be that of the wind,
your compactness
that of the forest.

孫子兵法

> **"**
> If we do not wish to fight, we can prevent the enemy from engaging us ... All we need do is to throw something odd and unaccountable in his way.
> **"**

66

In raiding and plundering be
like fire, in immovability like
a mountain.

99

孫子兵法

> **It is a military axiom not to advance uphill against the enemy, nor to oppose him when he comes downhill.**

Do not pursue an enemy who simulates flight; do not attack soldiers whose temper is keen.

孫子兵法

Do not swallow bait offered by the enemy. Do not interfere with an army that is returning home.

When you surround an army, leave an outlet free. Do not press a desperate foe too hard.

孫子兵法

> There are roads which must not be followed, armies which must be not attacked, towns which must not be besieged, positions which must not be contested, commands of the sovereign which must not be obeyed.

Reduce the hostile chiefs by
inflicting damage on them;
and make trouble for them,
and keep them constantly
engaged.

孫子兵法

"

On contentious ground,
attack not.

"

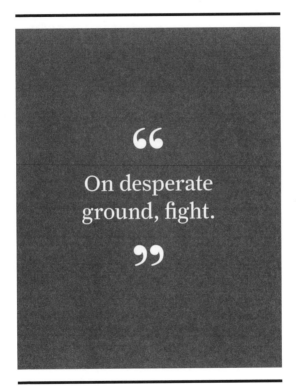

66

On desperate
ground, fight.

99

孫子兵法

> **66**
>
> Begin by seizing something which your opponent holds dear; then he will be amenable to your will.
>
> **99**

❝

Rapidity is the essence of war:
take advantage of the enemy's
unreadiness, make your way
by unexpected routes, and
attack unguarded spots.

❞

孫子兵法

66

When invading hostile
territory, the general principle
is, that penetrating deeply
brings cohesion; penetrating
but a short way means
dispersion.

99

If the enemy leaves
a door open, you
must rush in.

孫子兵法

> Exhibit the coyness of a maiden, until the enemy gives you an opening; afterwards emulate the rapidity of a running hare, and it will be too late for the enemy to oppose you.

66

If it is to your advantage, make a forward move; if not, stay where you are.

99

孫子兵法

CHAPTER

SIX

VICTORY

It goes without saying that the objective of battle is to emerge victorious. *The Art of War* teaches that the ultimate aim is a win that is quick, easy, and causes the least destruction to your foe. But the surest step on the road to victory is to secure yourself against defeat. And to win without fighting is the greatest victory of all.

孫子兵法

66

In war, then, let your great object be victory, not lengthy campaigns.

99

66

The best thing of all is to take
the enemy's country whole
and intact; to shatter and
destroy it is not so good.

99

孫子兵法

66

To fight and conquer in all your battles is not supreme excellence; supreme excellence consists in breaking the enemy's resistance without fighting.

99

He will win who
knows when to
fight and when
not to fight.

孫子兵法

> **He will win who knows how to handle both superior and inferior forces.**

"

He will win whose army is
animated by the same spirit
throughout all its ranks.

"

孫子兵法

> 66
>
> He will win who,
> prepared himself,
> waits to take the
> enemy unprepared.
>
> 99

66

He will win who has military capacity and is not interfered with by the sovereign.

99

孫子兵法

66

The good fighters of old first put themselves beyond the possibility of defeat, and then waited for an opportunity of defeating the enemy.

99

"

To secure ourselves against defeat lies in our own hands, but the opportunity of defeating the enemy is provided by the enemy himself.

"

孫子兵法

> **The good fighter is able to secure himself against defeat, but cannot make certain of defeating the enemy.**

Ability to defeat the
enemy means taking
the offensive.

孫子兵法

> **"**
> What the ancients called
> a clever fighter is one who
> not only wins, but excels in
> winning with ease.
> **"**

66

Making no mistakes is what
establishes the certainty
of victory, for it means
conquering an enemy that
is already defeated.

99

孫子兵法

66

You can be sure of succeeding in your attacks if you only attack places which are undefended. You can ensure the safety of your defense if you only hold positions that cannot be attacked.

99

66

He who can modify his tactics
in relation to his opponent and
thereby succeed in winning,
may be called a heaven-born
captain.

99

孫子兵法

66

In war, practice dissimulation
and you will succeed.

99

He will conquer who
has learnt the artifice
of deviation.

孫子兵法

> **"**
> If you know the enemy and know yourself, your victory will not stand in doubt; if you know Heaven and know Earth, you may make your victory complete.
> **"**